DATE DUE

JAN 23			
FEB 27			
MAR 5			
APR 25 '79			
OCT 17			
NOV 1	7		
OCT 3			

C.1-2

E
M

Mizumura, Kazue
If I built a village
X20060

If I Built a Village …

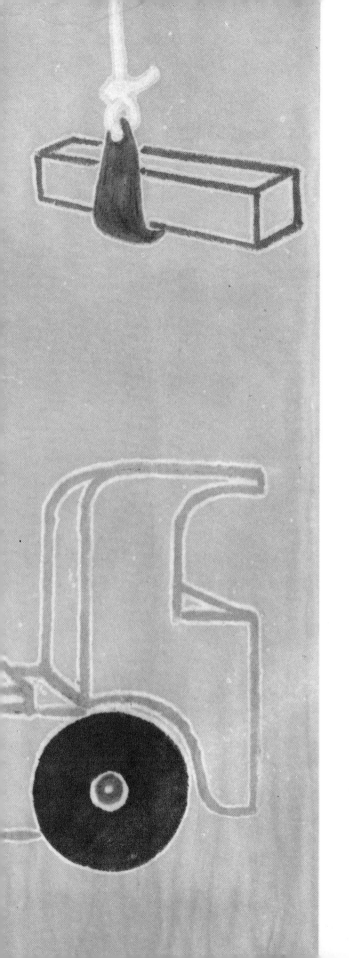

If I Built a Village...

By Kazue Mizumura

Thomas Y. Crowell Company

New York

BY THE AUTHOR

The Blue Whale
The Emperor Penguins
If I Built a Village...
If I Were a Mother...
I See the Winds
The Way of an Ant

Designed by Kazue Mizumura

Manufactured in the United States of America

L.C. Card 77-140645
ISBN 0-690-42903-7
0-690-42904-5 (LB)

2   3   4   5   6   7   8   9   10

A Jérôme et Denis en Iverny

If I built a village
Upon the hill
Along the river
In the woods,

There would be rabbits
Leaping in the sun,
Their white tails
A streak and a flash
Against the wind.

There would be trout
That shine like rainbows
Swimming in the river
As their shadows
Flicker and swirl
Through the ripples.

There would be owls, too,
For me to listen to when they hoot
In the woods at night,
Their eyes full of
Moon lights.

If I built a town
In the valleys
Around the lakes
Beside the forests,

I would leave the jumping mice
Sound asleep
In their nests,
Deep under the frosted valley,
Until the spring melts the ice.

And I would welcome the geese
From Canada
As they line grandly
On the lake,
To glide in and out
Of the drifting mist.

I would keep quiet for the deer
Tasting the raindrops
Scattered from the fiddleheads
In the forest.

If I built a city
By the sea,
Beneath the ground,
High against the sky,

There would be whales' spouts
Fountain high,
Far out at sea
Sprinkling pearl sprays
Over the Northern Lights.

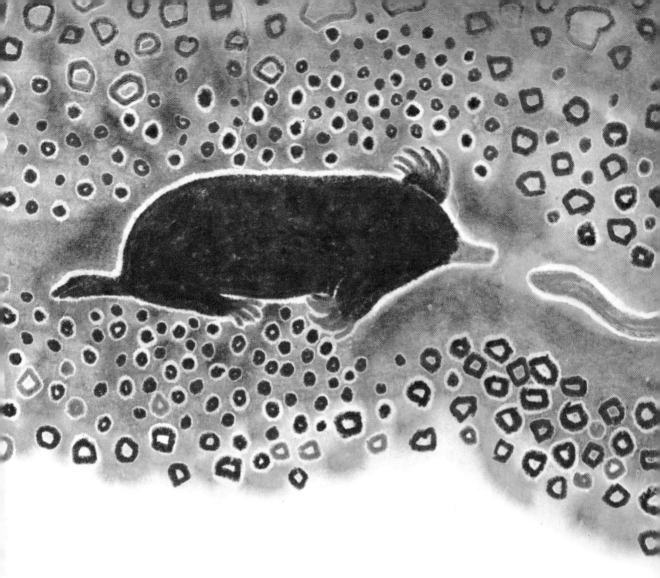

There would be moles
Seeking their meals along the tunnels
Where the fallen leaves
Turn into earth
Soft and dark.

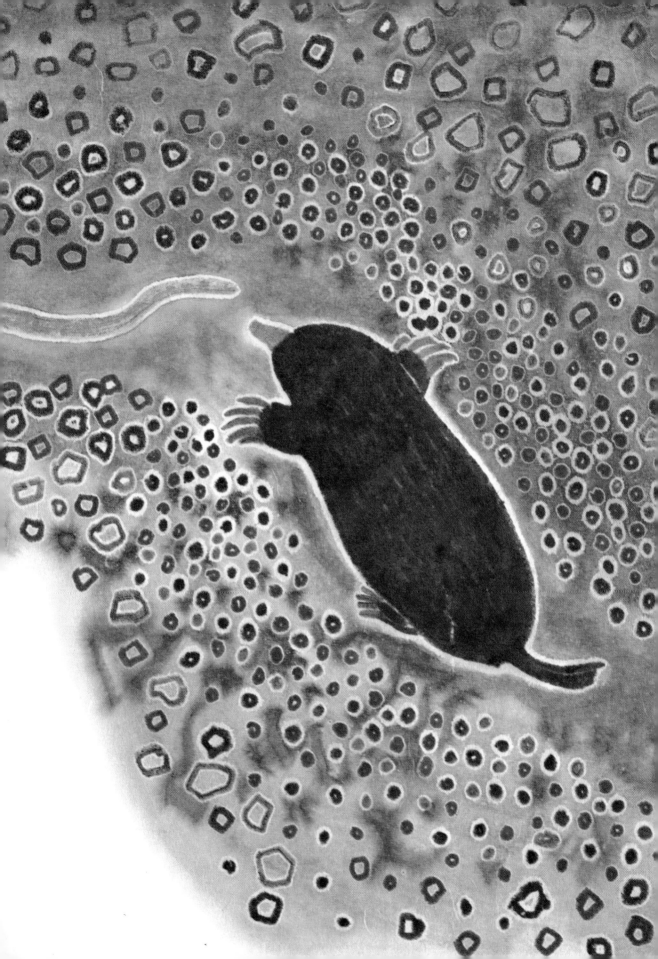

And there would be eagles
To soar to the sky
With their wings
Spread and still
Amid the summer clouds
As long as they wished.

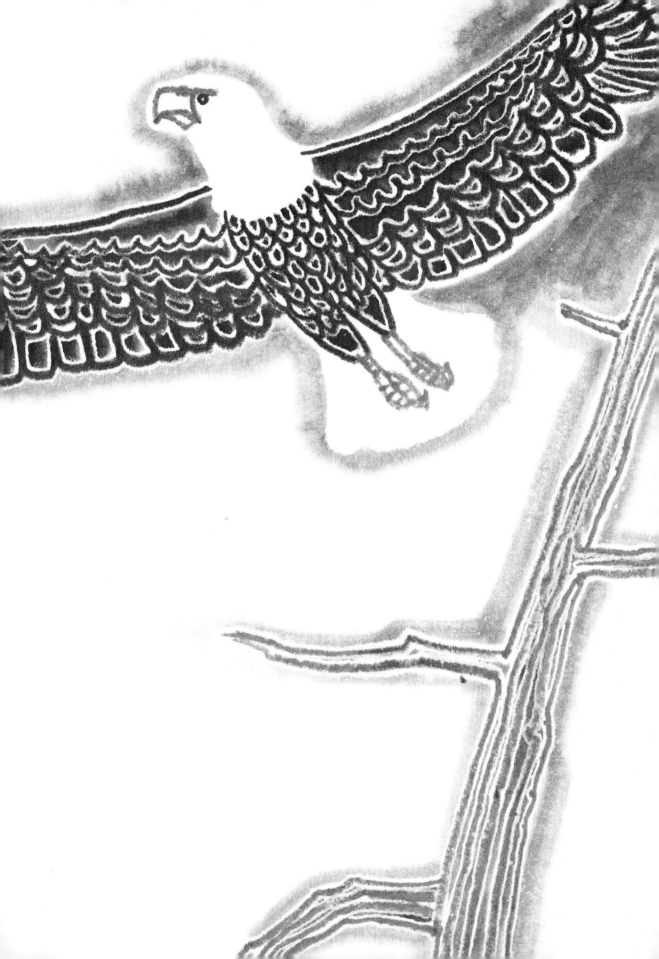

If I built my village,
My town and my city—
There would be people
Who would care and share
With all living things
The land they love.

ABOUT KAZUE MIZUMURA

Kazue Mizumura is a well-known illustrator and jacket artist for both children's and adult books. She is also both author and illustrator of a number of books for young readers. Busy as she is, Miss Mizumura still finds time for Japanese brush drawing and for jewelry design.

Born in Kamakura, Japan, Miss Mizumura studied at the Women's Art Institute in Tokyo and at Pratt Institute in Brooklyn, New York. She lives in Stamford, Connecticut.